creepy creatures

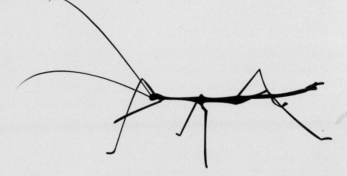

Published by Creative Paperbacks
P.O. Box 227, Mankato, Minnesota 56002
Creative Paperbacks is an imprint of
The Creative Company
www.thecreativecompany.us

Design by Ellen Huber
Production by Chelsey Luther
Art direction by Rita Marshall
Printed in the United States of America

Photographs by Dreamstime (Hans-peter Egert,
Isselee, Sascha Preußner), Getty Images (David
Barrie, Visuals Unlimited, Inc./Alex Wild, Hein
von Horsten, Kevin Schafer), iStockphoto (Evgeniy
Ayupov, JULIEN CADOT, Eric Isselée, TommyIX),
Shutterstock (Andrew Burgess, Melinda Fawver,
IrinaK, Eric Isselee, David W. Leindecker, Madlen,
rck_953), SuperStock (Animals Animals, Imagemore,
Minden Pictures, Tier und Naturfotografie)

Library of Congress Cataloging-in-Publication Data
Bodden, Valerie.
Stick insects / Valerie Bodden.
p. cm. — (Creepy creatures)
Summary: A basic introduction to stick insects,
examining where they live, how they grow, what
they eat, and the unique traits that help to define
them, such as their ability to hide on plants.
Includes bibliographical references and index.
ISBN 978-1-60818-359-3 (hardcover)
ISBN 978-0-89812-938-0 (pbk)
1. Stick insects—Juvenile literature. I. Title. II.
Series: Bodden, Valerie. Creepy creatures.
QL509.5.B63 2014
595.7'29—dc23   2013009756

First Edition
9 8 7 6 5 4 3 2 1

CONTENTS

stick insects

VALERIE BODDEN

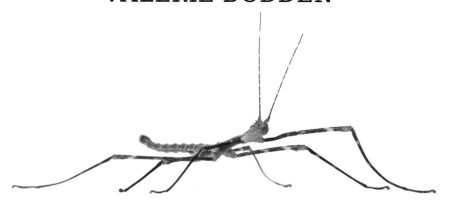

CREATIVE
PAPER BACKS

You are walking through the woods. You think you see a stick crawling up a tree. You look closer.

It is a stick insect!

Stick insects are also called walkingsticks. They are some of the longest insects in the world. Stick insects have three body parts and six legs. They have two **antennae** (*an-TEH-nee*). Some stick insects have two pairs of wings.

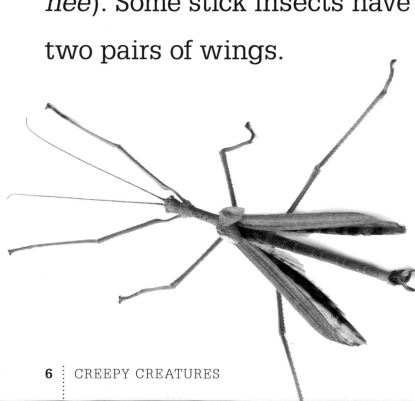

Stick insects that live on the ground do not need wings

Some stick insects are very long, but most are 3 inches (7.6 cm)

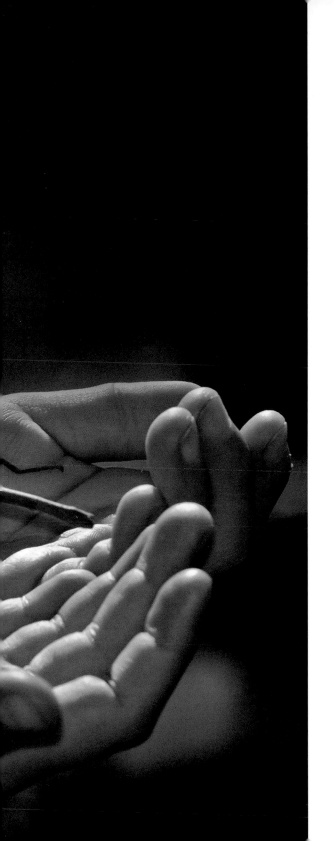

Most stick insects are brown or green. They are long and thin like a stick. Some are thorny or spiny. The smallest stick insects are as long as your thumb-nail. The biggest are longer than a ruler!

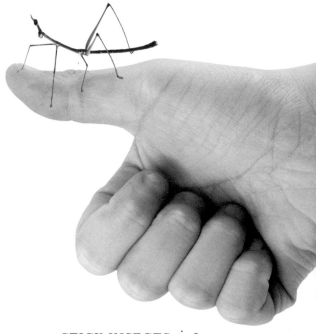

There are about 2,500 kinds of stick insects. The northern walkingstick is common in North America. Goliath stick insects live in Australia. These big stick insects have spines on their legs.

Both northern walkingsticks (pictured) and goliath stick insects (left) live in forests

A stick insect stays still to trick predators into thinking it's just a stick

Many stick insects live in rainforests. Some make their home in grasslands or deserts.

Stick insects have to watch out for **predators**. Lizards, birds, and mice all eat stick insects.

Stick insects begin life in eggs. **Nymphs** (*NIMFS*) hatch from the eggs. The nymphs look like small adult stick insects without wings. As the nymphs grow, they **molt**. After they molt five or six times, the nymphs become adults. Adult stick insects live from three months to more than a year.

A female stick insect can lay up to 1,500 eggs at a time

Stick insects use powerful jaws called mandibles to eat leaves

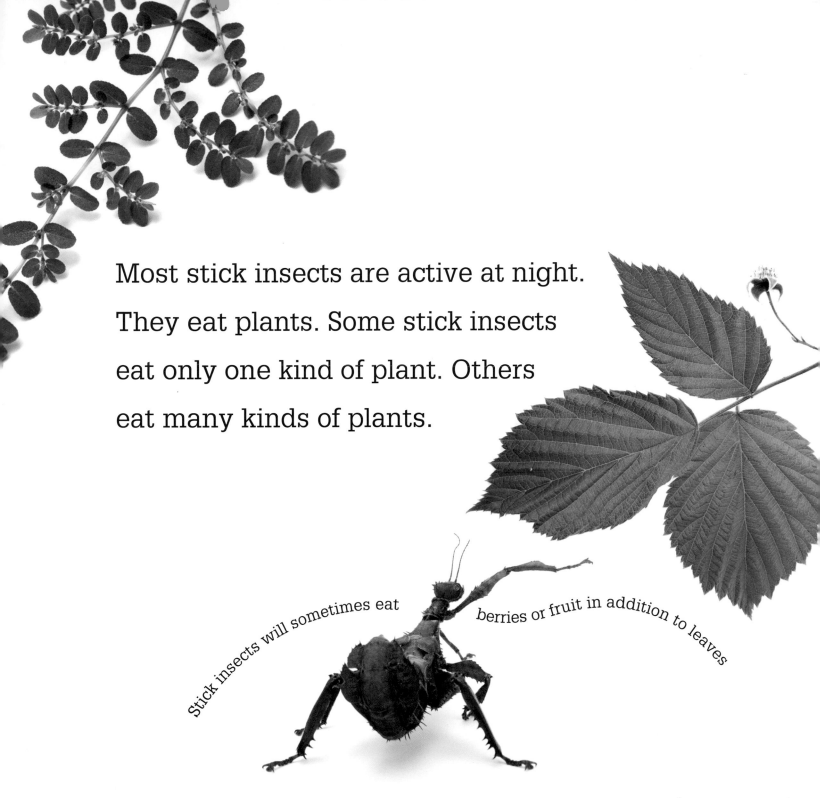

Most stick insects are active at night. They eat plants. Some stick insects eat only one kind of plant. Others eat many kinds of plants.

Stick insects will sometimes eat berries or fruit in addition to leaves

Stick insects are good at hiding on plants. They hold very still. When they have to move, they might sway to look like a twig blowing in the wind. Some stick insects can squirt bad-smelling liquids. Stick insects can break off a leg if a predator grabs it.

Some stick insects look like leaves or other plant parts

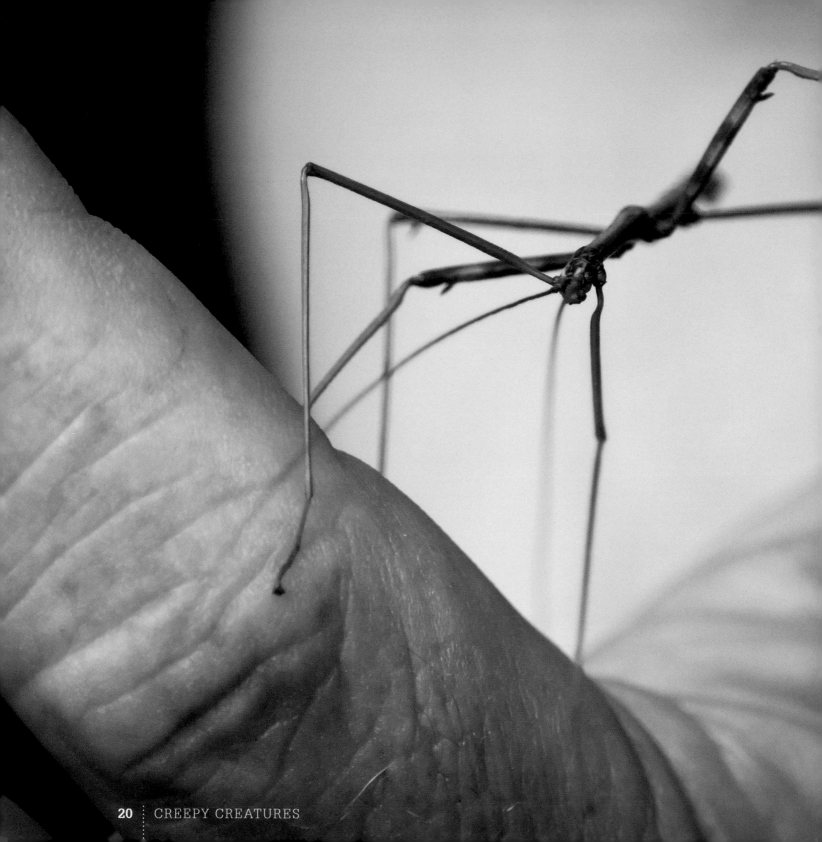

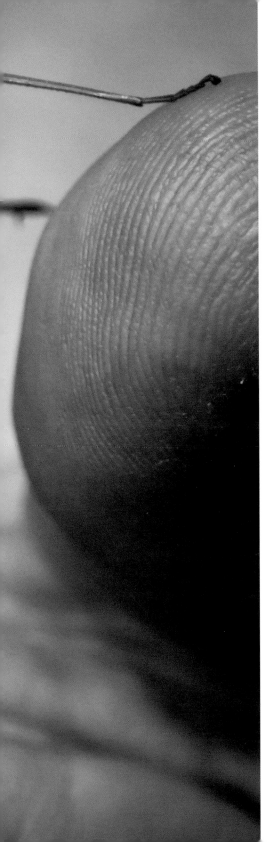

Some people keep big stick insects as pets. They have to be careful not to get poked if the stick insect has spines. It can be fun to watch these stick-shaped creepy creatures walk around!

Stick insects can make good pets because they move slowly and do not bite

MAKE A STICK INSECT

You can make a stick insect out of a real stick and some pipe cleaners. First, find a long, thin stick from outside. Wrap the middle of a pipe cleaner around the stick to make two legs (one on each side of the stick). Do the same thing with two more pipe cleaners. Bend each leg in the middle to make your stick insect stand!

GLOSSARY

antennae: feelers on the heads of some insects that are used to touch, smell, and taste things

molt: to lose a shell or layer of skin and grow a new, larger one

nymphs: young stick insects

predators: animals that kill and eat other animals

READ MORE

Green, Emily K. *Walkingsticks.* Minneapolis: Bellwether Media, 2007.

Richardson, Adele. *Walking Sticks.* North Mankato, Minn.: Smart Apple Media, 1999.

WEBSITES

Enchanted Learning: Walkingstick
http://www.enchantedlearning.com/ subjects/insects/orthoptera/ Indianwalkingstick.shtml

Learn more about stick insects, and print out a picture to color.

Pets: Stick Insect Care Advice
http://www.petsathome.com/webapp/wcs/ stores/servlet/Info_10601_caring-for-your-stick-insect_-1_10551

Learn about keeping stick insects as pets.